MLK Jr.'s
Detroit Dream

Memoir of a Civil Rights Foot Soldier

SHARON ELIZABETH SEXTON

NEWMAN SPRINGS PUBLISHING
320 Broad Street
Red Bank, NJ 07701

First originally published by Newman Springs Publishing 2023

ISBN 979-8-88763-380-0 (Paperback)
ISBN 979-8-88763-381-7 (Digital)

Printed in the United States of America

Sexton Family Portrait, 1963

From left to right:
Mrs. Josephine Elizabeth Adams-Sexton
Sharon Elizabeth Sexton
William Niles Sexton, Jr.
Lt. Col. William N. Sexton, Sr.

It was only two weeks from my ninth birthday. The day was a bright and warm Sunday, June 23, 1963, and my daddy told me we were going to a parade.

I liked the parades!

My mom dressed me in a pretty Sunday summer dress. I didn't like dresses and thought it was a strange outfit for a parade.

My older brother and father both wore ties. My dad even had on a dress suit, like he was going to work or church. My mom wore a suit too, and a fancy hat whose color matched her purse and shoes.

During the car ride downtown, Mom explained that we were going to see Dr. Martin Luther King Jr.

"Ain't he the one causing trouble down South?" I asked, familiar with the name "King" because I saw the news reports on TV, showing black people getting beaten in the streets of southern cities, and a Negro minister (we called ourselves Negroes back then) named Reverend King was trying to stop it.

"The question is, *is*," my mother, who was a teacher, scolded me. "Not *ain't*, and the trouble Dr. King is causing is he's fighting for our peoples' rights and doing it nonviolently," Mother corrected me.

My dad added, "And it's the twentieth anniversary of a problem we had in Detroit. Back then, black and white folk didn't get along as well as they do today. There was an argument between the two groups at Belle Isle, and the argument went into the streets, and the two sides fought for three days. People were killed, and the city was left in shambles. Dr. King is coming here to see our progress. So we're going to be on our best behavior today. Right?"

"Right," my brother and I answered in unison.

I knew that the parade we were going to see was fancy. When we drove into downtown Detroit and saw the crowds of people walking on the sidewalks toward Woodward Avenue and Cobo Hall, I had never seen so many people. According to the news reports later that day, my family was among an estimated 150-thousand civil rights activists crammed into a sea of humanity to hear one man speak.

The people represented every race who lived in the city, from dark and light-skinned, people-of-color to white people of every ethnicity. Little kids younger than me were being carried by their parents, and old people in wheelchairs were being rolled in sync with the movement of the walkers.

I was swept along the sidewalk with the current of feet and held onto my parents' hands so we wouldn't get separated. Finally, we stopped because we could go no further. The wall of people in front of us was solid, and where we stood was to be our spot for the rest of the day.

From my position in the crowd, I was looking at adults' waists and could only hear a faint rumble as the crowd around me got excited. My dad reached down and had me climb up on his shoulders, something I hadn't done since I was three. When my dad rose up, so did I, and I could see over the heads of the grown-ups.

My mom was pointing and said, "Here they come."

I looked, but all I could see were more people!

HUDSON
DEPARTMENT STORE
Equality
Strong House Laws
LAW support ALL
Fight for FREEDOM
Together we can!

The "more people" were a line of men, like a wall, walking in an unbreakable force across the entire width of Woodward Avenue. Their arms were locked at the elbows, and they were chanting while singing.

"We shall ooov-er coooo-mee."

"We shall ooov-er coooo-mee."

"We shall ooov-er coooo-mee, soooome-dayyyyie."

I looked again. No clowns. No big balloons. No floats.

"What kind of parade was this?" I asked myself.

"Look! There is Reverend King!" My mom pointed.

"Where?" I asked.

"In the middle."

There, in the middle of the line of men who all looked alike in their dark suits, ties, and hats, was a brown-skinned man with a kind face and excited eyes. He sort of looked like my own dad.

King and his line of leaders marched past us as they led row after row of mostly black men, with a few whites, and women scattered in the mass of might. They made a mosaic of faces determined to change America as they passed by.

Then more rows of people marched past but dressed alike in union uniforms representing their auto plants or factory affiliations that fueled the Motor City. Then the church people started marching by in their church groups.

"Look, Bill!" my mom shouted to my dad. "There's your mother with the Plymouth Church Group."

My mom pointed to the banner holding the Plymouth Congregational Church sign.

My mom, usually a very reserved woman, started waving her arms widely above her head as she shouted Grandma Connie's name, trying to get her attention.

Finally, the last of the marchers stopped in front of us because they had nowhere else to advance. The throng of marchers now comprised the standing audience that had enveloped Woodward Avenue. Only a sea of smiling faces could be seen in every direction as my dad, once again, placed me up on his shoulders so I could be above the bodies that were closing in on me.

We stood there in one place for hours as the keynote speakers' voices boomed through the powerful public address system that had been constructed for the occasion.

For an almost nine-year-old, the messages from the voices were literarily over my head. But the crowd cheered at almost everything that was said, and then a very powerful voice hushed the crowd.

"That's Dr. King," my mom informed me.

I liked his voice. It was soothing, I thought, as he talked to the crowd, mesmerizing it with his Baptist preacher inflections and historical truths.

"I have a dream," boomed Dr. King's voice as the already standing crowd tried to stand taller to get a better look at the speakers that electrified the big voice that made everyone stand at attention.

"I have a dream," said Dr. King again as the audience reacted with claps and shouts of "Yes."

To me, Dr. King's dream didn't seem too far-fetched. It seemed to me that he wasn't asking for too much. I felt I could help Dr. King fulfill his dream!

"Free at last. Free at last. Thank God almighty, we are free at last!"

By the end of King's speech, I, too, was on my toes, clapping and shouting and happy. I was going to be a foot soldier in the war against oppression, despair, and segregation!

A few months later, on August 28, Dr. King marched on Washington, DC, the same way he came to Detroit. I learned that the activities in the nation's capital were to be televised, and I, along with my family, was glued to the television that Wednesday afternoon.

Since King had left Detroit, I had watched his civil rights progress on the nightly news. Dr. King was trying to convince prejudiced people that black folks were nice. I couldn't understand why some people hated me and my family simply because our skin was a different color than theirs.

I couldn't understand why some parents didn't want me to go to school with their children. I wasn't going to hurt them. I didn't even have to talk to them or play with them or eat with them or go to the movies with them.

I just wanted to be able to do my schoolwork without being afraid of others being mean to me. I just wanted to go to a clean school where teachers thought I was worth teaching. I just wanted to grow up dreaming the way Dr. King dreamed of a little black girl reaching her potential.

The march on Washington was like watching the march on Detroit all over again but on television. The massive Washington, DC, crowd was impressive.

To my surprise, Dr. King repeated his "I Have a Dream" speech to the nation. Again, the crowd was mesmerized. Again, at nine years old, I was committed to being a foot soldier in the civil rights movement, but my mom wouldn't let me go south to be a student activist. She said I was too young. So I had to be satisfied watching the civil rights movement on the nightly news as Dr. King and his followers marched across the South, meeting resistance to their peaceful, nonviolent plea to have all the rights of an American.

As a young person, my portal into the outer world was through the television screen. My mom bought a set of TV-trays so I could eat in the family room while watching television. My grandma said my mom was spoiling me. Grandma told my mom that she was using the television to babysit me, and that the violence on television was a bad influence. Mostly out of respect, I couldn't tell grandma she was wrong. The fact of the matter was, I just liked to watch television, and I watched everything. Cartoons were my favorite, and I must admit that I loved spinach because Popeye-the-Sailorman got his superpowers from a can of spinach! I also watched game shows, kid shows, old monster movies, nature programs, comedy sitcoms, and I really liked television westerns.

On Sunday nights, a variety program called The Ed Sullivan Show featured every kind of animal act, popular singers, dance performances, various musical instrumental styles, and was every week, a television event. Everyone I knew, even my dad, watched the show because occasionally, it would feature one of the American black artists or entertainers who were popular at the time. All of my parents' friends would call one another on the telephone to remind each other to watch The Ed Sullivan Show when a person-of-color was going to be featured.

One Sunday, I couldn't believe my eyes. There, on The Ed Sullivan Show was the blind black boy who was in my brother's class at Fitzgerald Elementary School. I knew he lived on Greenlawn Street because I would see him when I walked past his mama's house. I also remembered seeing him in school reading a lesson from his braille schoolbook. Now, I watched him on TV as he played the harmonica with the same fingers he used to touch and read the braille bumps in the school book!

"Little Stevie Wonder from Detroit, Michigan", Ed Sullivan said as he introduced the world to Motown Records' newest talent who happened to be my neighbor and schoolmate. The Motown Records label was Michigan's only record studio. It specialized in a unique sound that was making the City of Detroit famous for something other than manufacturing cars. Plus, Motown was an

African American owned and operated company that discovered, developed, and promoted local black talent getting into the entertainment business.

That night, in a rare display of spontaneous joy on national television, the live, enthusiastic, interracial theater audience jumped out of their seats to dance with one another and clap along with Stevie Wonder's premiere performance. The brief image on the television screen filled with happy black and white faces reacting to the music, seemed natural. "I bet they cut 'that' out the show 'down south'", my mom said with a sarcastic grin referring to the censures who would block out the integrated dance segments of the program when it aired in southern states.

On the television screens in the rest of the country the picture was an up-close shot on Stevie's small but sturdy, 13-year-old body in a tailored made man-suit which made him look, almost grown. Everyone watching that night, forgot Stevie was without eyesight as he bopped up and down or swayed to the sweet rhythms that were coming from his harmonica in between the delightful lyrics of 'Fingertips'.

That night, I was proud to be a black person. Proud to be from Detroit. And proud to be from my neighborhood.

I could see, Stevie was fulfilling Reverend King's dream of bringing people together, "and he is blind!", I thought to myself. Then I realized, I can do something special too. But what? Cause I couldn't sing!

As the 1960s progressed, watching television news programs was sometimes scary. The news showed the civil rights activists in the south being abused by white people who didn't want to integrate. Children my age who wanted to go to better schools were being beaten and made to stay away. In fact, three little girls who could have been my friends were killed in a church bombing on a Sunday morning while at church! My mom would shake her head with a tear in her eye as she watched the reports, point her finger to the screen and say, "that's why you can't be a freedom rider!"

VOLCANO
HUMAN
BRAIN

The racial hate, however, wasn't confined to the South. On my own block in Detroit, an incident happened that same summer that sent shivers up my spine. One night, I was home alone on Cherrylawn Street in northwest Detroit. My street was integrated with a few black families, Jewish people, and immigrants from Europe, but most of our neighbors were white Americans. I was watching television when I heard a loud sound from outside. When I went to the front side window to investigate, what I saw brought the South onto my street and into my safety zone. Glowing in orange and red was a giant cross in flames that were burning on my elderly Jewish neighbor's lawn.

Although it was strangely beautiful, I knew what it meant. I ducked my head low enough in the window not to be seen from the outside but high enough to watch the front of my own house to see if any movement was going to burn a cross on our lawn. I thought to myself, *What kind of people are these?* A little of my innocence disappeared that night.

As I grew into a preteen, the civil rights struggle had its own growing pains, like the assignation of John F. Kennedy, the president of the United States, on November 4, 1963. Kennedy had been moving the civil rights struggle into the mainstream of the American consciousness when he was slain. His death put a pause in the movement's momentum.

Then there were the civil rights student marchers in the South, where the young black people tried to eat at the counters of restaurants, but they were beaten up by white adults. That made me mad, but my mom still wouldn't let me go and help the college students in Alabama, Mississippi, and Louisiana, who were also going door-to-door to get people registered to vote. I had to watch the students, some my own age, getting sprayed with fire hoses and attacked by police dogs on my television set like it was a nightly horror movie in my living room. The struggle, while being televised, was also being violently resisted by horrible people, screaming nasty and untrue words at children my age trying to go to school and get an education.

Next was the assassination of Malcolm X on February 21, 1965. Malcolm X was the polar opposite of Dr. King in tactics concerning civil rights in America. Malcolm X was a former follower of the Honorable Elijah Muhammad, a former editor of the *Muhammad Speaks Newspaper*, and a former spokesperson for the Nation of Islam, which was a black Muslim religious sect. Malcolm X presented his opinions in a fiery expression of political thought that justified its tactics "by any means necessary."

BREAKING NEWS!
Children killed in Alabama Church bombing

Malcolm X's speeches captured the imagination of black America, unlike King's more subdued approach to fighting back against racial oppression. Malcolm X and Dr. King were often pitted against each other in the media as opposition leaders for the heart and soul of the black community. After Malcolm X's split with the Nation of Islam, he went on a cultural and religious trip to Mecca in Saudi Arabia for the Hajj, a Muslim religious quest, and came back with an enlightened awareness and a new name, Malik El-Shabazz. But Malcolm X's tragic death shocked America and brought an emergency to the plight of the black community. I remember watching the news reports announcing Malcolm X's demise and didn't understand the sadness that overcame me. Malcolm X's death made me grow up a little and did spark a fire in me of resistance to oppression by any means necessary, even if it cost my own life!

Malcolm X and his rhetoric of black pride gave birth to the Black Power Movement of the 1960s. Pride in black and African culture led to changes in black people's style in clothing, hair, and attitude. Afro hairstyles became popular, African prints in clothing fabrics were being worn, and one's own clenched fist in the air was the *community* unifying personal expression, and the phrase "Black Power" became an empowering slogan. I, too, sang along with the godfather of soul, James Brown, repeating, "Say it loud, I'm Black, and I'm proud," and singing along with songstress Nina Simone, who made being "Young, Gifted, and Black" a way of life for African American youth, as well as an anthem.

In the black community, everyone was watching a young, brash, conceded, handsome, black boxer named Cassius Clay, who went from a boxing sensation at the 1960 Summer Olympics to a nonconsecutive, three-time heavyweight champion title holder by the end of his career twenty years later. During the height of his popularity and championship accomplishments, Clay joined the Nation of Islam under the influence of Malcolm X, changed his name to Muhammad Ali, refused to fight in the Vietnam War, in which the United States was heavily militarily engaged, went to jail for his beliefs, and emerged as a hero in the eyes of black America and the African world of black people.

Ali's stance on not fighting in a war stemmed from the fact that the Vietnamese enemy was not his enemy. Ali protested that black soldiers, who were a minority in their own country, were sent to the front lines of white America's war to be the majority of the wounded and then sent back home to a land of discrimination and segregation. My own father could identify with that fact being a WWII veteran and never having gotten the incentives and perks that the white soldiers got returning from fighting in the same war for European freedom.

Even Dr. King started to preach against the war. King's turnabout on the Vietnam War angered many against him, criticizing King and calling him unappreciative of their support.

At about this same time, a group of black youth and young adults started the Black Panther Party, which was like a political organization but became a paramilitary organization that was comprised of mostly African American young people who armed themselves to protect the community against racist police and what they perceived as violent attacks by outsiders. Although their actions were villainized by the police and sensationalized on the nightly news, the Panthers also started anti-hunger and community health programs that were later continued by the US government. I personally knew members of Detroit's Black Panther Party and didn't see them as dangerous people but as classmates who took pride in the community. My parents, on the other hand, believed the news stories and forbade me to socialize with obvious Panther members who wore black beret hats on their heads, military garb, and looked mean. I still bought their newspaper because, as a pre-teenage girl, I thought the Black Panthers were "brave" and "cute."

During the years, there were also achievements in the civil rights struggle that broke new ground, like national laws that the newest President Lyndon B. Johnson pushed in Congress with the support of Dr. King, that established the Civil Rights and Voter Rights legislation. During this time, the violence against the students in the South stopped as a national reaction to the violence began to support the civil rights efforts. In addition, the segregation signs in the South that spewed racial insults like "no ni--ers" or "whites only" came down, and blacks were allowed to shop and eat wherever they could afford to go.

As a country, we seemed to be on our way to fulfilling King's dream.

But on a Sunday afternoon, July 23, 1967, a little more than a week after my thirteenth birthday, my brother was playing a boring game of Little League Baseball when I wandered to the other side of the playground to the swing set. I was swinging on one of the swings behind the Olympia Ice-Skating Stadium on West Grand Boulevard and Grand River Avenue. From my perch on the swing, I could see black smoke billowing up into the sky, not far away. Then I saw another billow of black smoke in a different place in the sky, not far from the first line of smoke, and I heard the fire engine sirens getting louder. Then there were a lot of fire engine sirens coming from different directions and more billows of smoke rising in the skies not far from the park. I looked around, and my father was motioning and yelling at me, "Come on!"

24

When we got home, the local television news reports said that people were rioting in the City of Detroit, something about a police raid that went bad. For three days, the city was paralyzed as rioters and police fought in the streets. More than fifty people lost their lives, and hundreds of businesses were looted and burned as a result.

Grandma Connie lived not far from the riot zone. When my family went to check on her, we drove past National Guard Troops, who were called into the city to help stop the riot. The National Guard was camped down the street from my grandma's house on the Central High School playground with army tanks, troop buses, and other army equipment. The troops who patrolled the area were wearing handguns and holding rifles. They were ready for war!

I wondered who they were going to blow up with the cannons on the tanks. It was scary!

After that, many white people in Detroit moved to the suburbs. My parents, who had been looking for a new house, were suddenly able to qualify for a home mortgage loan. They were also shown houses in neighborhoods that had been denied to them in the past. When my family moved into our new house, my dad laughed at the clause in the paperwork that said he could not have "Negroes" in the house after dark.

On April 4, 1968, a little short of five years after King's march on Detroit, I was thirteen years old and participating in my Beaubien Junior High School program that celebrated African American culture, arts, and history. My classmate David was reciting Dr. Martin Luther King Jr.'s "I Have a Dream" speech, which had become a favorite speech for school programs.

David didn't go on the program as rehearsed. Instead, his performance was moved to the end of the show. When David finally gave King's speech, he was wonderful. It was the best interpretation of the speech I had ever heard. David, that night, was great and so expressive. It was just like Dr. King had come into David through him.

I have a
dream...

When David completed King's speech, the school principal announced that Dr. Rev. Martin Luther King Jr. had been shot at a hotel in Memphis, Tennessee. In two minutes, the auditorium was empty.

For the next twenty-four hours, America was in shock and reeling from the assassination of Dr. King.

I was sad, very, very sad.

I couldn't remember that time today without a tear in my eye.

We, as a nation, could have given up on the march for civil rights. Yes, there were people who acted badly by rioting and causing violence and terminal where they lived. But more people decided to take King's mission into their own hearts and do good works.

Eventually, segregation laws were abolished in the South. Schools all over the country were integrated. Retail establishments were forced to open their doors to people of color. Black people could finally vote in political elections without restrictions in most of America. Opportunities in higher education and employment opened in many places for people of color, and I grew up hoping to take advantage of the opportunities that had not been available to my parents.

Today, I am still a foot soldier in the struggle for civil rights because the job isn't over, and there is still much work to be accomplished. We, as American people, cannot become complacent and satisfied with how things are now because we are not where Dr. Martin Luther King Jr. envisioned us to be—yet!

Sharon E. Sexton, 1963

Sharon E. Sexton, 1968

March photos taken by
W.N. Sexton Sr., June 23, 1963

Sharon & brother on front doorstep
before leaving for '63 March

Sharon E. Sexton and her
puppy Dagwood, 1963

ABOUT THE AUTHOR

Sharon Elizabeth Sexton is the only daughter of Lieutenant Colonel (retired) William N. Sexton Sr. and Josephine E. Adams-Sexton of Detroit, Michigan. Because of her father's military affiliation, as a child, Miss Sexton traveled with her parents and brother, living in Europe and Asia. After the Sexton family settled in Detroit, Michigan, Ms. Sexton's love of writing, telling stories, and interpreting history began.

During her senior year of high school, Ms. Sexton won the Miss Black Teenage America Pageant, 1971–1972. She was then even more dedicated to uplifting her people. With a degree in racial and ethnic studies and another in telecommunications from Michigan State University, Ms. Sexton developed her award-winning television investigative reporting skills to research African American history around the country. After twenty years in broadcasting, Ms. Sexton moved her engaging storytelling way to reconstruct African American history into other disciplines, which included monument building.

In 1996, Ms. Sexton initiated the concept of building two monuments dedicated to the underground railroad on both sides of the Detroit River, one in Canada and the other in the USA. She then created and led a nonprofit organization, the International Underground Railroad Monument Collaborative, to partner with Detroit 300, which built the two monuments. The Gateway to Freedom (USA) and The Tower of Freedom (Canada) were dedicated to the Underground Railroad for Detroit's three hundredth founding anniversary in 2001.

Ms. Sexton, also a documentary filmmaker, has produced and directed an internationally acclaimed anthology of Detroit's early African American history entitled *Black Bottom and Paradise Valley, the Forgotten Legacy*. Over the years, Ms. Sexton has authored several articles about African American history for national newspapers and magazines. She has also developed a youth-orientated elementary school presentation to engage youth in social action activities. Ms. Sexton is passing her skills on to the following generations by teaching young adults with an interest in their ancestors and her investigative techniques for researching black history.

As cofounder and the executive director of research for the Michigan Underground Railroad Exploratory Collective (MUREC), which is affiliated with the Charles H. Wright Museum of African American History, and as the current Chairperson of the Black Historic Sites Committee, which is affiliated with the Detroit Historical Museum, Ms. Sexton will continue to produce positive, accurate, and informative African American history presentations for future generations.